Tequila

COCKTAILS

Tequila

COCKTAILS

Over 40 tequila and mezcal-based
drinks from around the world

JESSE ESTES

PHOTOGRAPHY BY
ALEX LUCK

RYLAND PETERS & SMALL
LONDON • NEW YORK

To my family, for being a continual source of support and inspiration.

Notes:

- Each cocktail recipe serves 1 person unless otherwise stated
- Use Maldon sea salt where possible
- Edible flowers must be food-safe and pesticide-free
- Raw egg white should not be fed to the very young, pregnant, elderly or anyone with a compromised immune system

Senior Designer Barbara Zuñiga
Editor Alice Sambrook
Head of Production Patricia Harrington
Editorial Director Julia Charles
Creative Director Leslie Harrington

Drinks Stylist Lorna Brash
Prop Stylist Luis Peral
Indexer Vanessa Bird

Cover illustration by Colin Elgie

First published in 2018 as *Tequila Beyond Sunrise*. This revised edition published in 2023 by
Ryland Peters & Small
20–21 Jockey's Fields
London WC1R 4BW
and
341 E 116th Street
New York, 10029

www.rylandpeters.com

10 9 8 7 6 5 4 3 2 1

Text copyright © Jesse Estes 2018, 2023
Design, photographs and cover illustration
copyright © Ryland Peters & Small 2018, 2023

ISBN: 978-1-78879-505-0

A CIP record for this book is available from the British Library. US Library of Congress CIP data has been applied for.

Printed in China

FSC
www.fsc.org
MIX
Paper | Supporting responsible forestry
FSC® C008047

CONTENTS

INTRODUCTION

To call tequila a misunderstood spirit would be an understatement.

I have been lucky enough to travel the world leading seminars, tastings, trainings and masterclasses on agave spirits to both bar industry professionals and end-consumers alike. I like to lead with the question: 'Who here has had a bad experience with tequila that has made them swear off drinking it for the rest of their lives?' Usually, at least 75% of hands will go up; in many cases nearly the entire audience.

This is a common experience and one not to be easily dismissed. However, there has been a big movement in the last decade towards tequila cementing itself as a legitimate spirit category amongst the likes of vodka, gin, whisk(e)y, brandy, etc. Mezcal – tequila's older and more robust relative – has resurfaced as the hip and trendy new drink of millennials, not only in places like Mexico City and London, but across the world. While there are still some poorly made agave spirits in the market, I would argue that a well-crafted tequila or mezcal is as good as (if not better than) the best Scotches or Cognacs.

In this book, I aim to share my experience, knowledge and passion for tequila and mezcal, and to show off the versatility of these two extraordinary spirits when mixed in cocktails. The selected cocktails are a combination of classics, my own creations and a selection of some of my favourite cocktails from around the world.

Salud! Jesse Estes

ABOUT TEQUILA AND MEZCAL

Tequila and mezcal are made from the majestic agave plant, which is indigenous to the Americas. Local populations previously used the plant to make things such as rope, needle and thread, paper, paving for roads and thatching for roofs. The consumption of fermented agave juice (known as *pulque*) dates back thousands of years and it is likely to be the oldest alcoholic beverage of the Americas. Agave distillate (mezcal) probably goes back at least 500 years, and in the state of Jalisco (near the town of Tequila), mezcal evolved into what is now called tequila.

Tequila has an internationally recognized denomination of origin – in the same way that Cognac or Champagne have. The rules set out by the Tequila Regulatory Council include stipulation of the variety of agave plants used to make the drink and the region in which it must be produced. If the label states '100% Agave Tequila', then it is made only from the blue agave plant. If not, then up to 49% of the sugars can come from a raw material other than agave, such as sugar cane. All the tequilas and mezcals used in this book are 100% agave.

So, what are the major differences between tequila and mezcal?

- **Region:** Tequila can only be produced within five Mexican states, most comes from the state of Jalisco. Mezcal is allowed to be produced in nine states, the majority coming from Oaxaca.
- **Agave varieties used:** Tequila is restricted to just one variety – the blue agave – whereas mezcal can legally use a much wider variety of agaves, espadín being the most popular.
- **Production process:** While agaves used in tequila are usually cooked in steam ovens, many mezcals are pit-roasted below ground, which can impart a smoky flavour.
- **Alcohol by volume percentage:** While most tequilas tend to be consumed at between 35–40% ABV, mezcals will often be bottled at between 45–50% ABV.
- **Aging:** While barrel-aging is now common for tequilas, aging mezcal in wood isn't – purists will assert that the wood hides the coveted agave notes found naturally in the distillate.

Mixing with tequila and mezcal:

Historically, tequila and mezcal are underrepresented in bar books, with bartenders of the late 19th- and early to mid-20th–century favouring gin, brandy and whisk(e)y. However, most respected cocktail bars in major cities now have an ample selection of tequila and mezcal cocktails.

The Margarita is tequila's most famous mixed drink but interestingly it is not consumed in Mexico outside of tourist destinations. The Paloma and Batanga (pages 19 and 23) are much more popular libations in Mexico itself.

I would argue that many classic cocktails originally calling for other spirits as a base work well when adapted with tequila or mezcal. Several such 'twisted classics' are included in this book and I encourage you to experiment with creating and enjoying your own.

What makes tequila and mezcal special?

There are hundreds of varieties of the agave plant, with just one species (blue agave) used for tequila, and several dozen used for mezcal production. Blue agave takes about eight years to mature, while some varieties of agave used for mezcal can grow for up to 40 years before harvest. The growth cycle for other spirits' raw materials (such as grains, sugar cane and fruits) is much shorter. Years of basking under the hot Mexican sun and soaking up minerals from the earth gives agave spirits a deep flavour. Those who love tequila tend to favour it over other spirits for this unique flavour imparted by the agave, the feeling it gives them, and perhaps to some extent the 'image' surrounding tequila. I encourage people to enjoy it neat, out of a glass designed to highlight its aromas, sipped and savoured instead of as a shot or slammer. However, tequila is all about fun, and as such should not be taken too seriously. The versatility of these spirits is what makes them work so phenomenally well in cocktails and mixed drinks.

MARGARITAS

◆

CLASSIC MARGARITA

One of the most popular alcoholic mixed drinks in the world, the origins of this cocktail are - perhaps surprisingly - largely unknown. While there are different ways to serve the Margarita (on the rocks, straight up, with salt or without salt, frozen, etc.) the recipe below is my favourite permutation of this cocktail.

LIME WEDGE AND SEA SALT FLAKES, FOR THE GLASS RIM
50 ML/1⅔ FL OZ. OCHO BLANCO TEQUILA
25 ML/¾ FL OZ. FRESH LIME JUICE
25 ML/¾ FL OZ. COINTREAU

Rub the outer rim of a chilled margarita glass with a lime wedge. Dip the glass rim into the sea salt flakes, taking care that the salt remains on the outside of the glass. Add the rest of the drink ingredients to a cocktail shaker with cubed ice and shake hard. Double strain into the salt-rimmed margarita glass.

EIGHT PROMISES

I was served this perfectly balanced drink by Anton Regnéll at Supper restaurant in Stockholm. It's his truly delectable twist on the Margarita.

LIME WEDGE AND BLACK LAVA SALT, FOR THE GLASS RIM

35 ML/1¼ FL OZ. OCHO BLANCO TEQUILA

25 ML/¾ FL OZ. FRESH LIME JUICE

15 ML/½ FL OZ. ITALICUS ROSOLIO DI BERGAMOTTO LIQUEUR

15 ML/½ FL OZ. LEMONGRASS SYRUP*

Rub a lime wedge around the rim of a chilled coupe glass before dipping into the black lava salt. Shake the rest of the ingredients vigorously in a cocktail shaker with cubed ice and double strain into the salt-rimmed glass.

To make lemongrass syrup: 1 LITRE/4 CUPS WATER, 1 KG/5 CUPS CASTER/ GRANULATED SUGAR, 5 BRUISED LEMONGRASS STALKS Add all ingredients to saucepan and bring mixture to a boil. Remove from heat and stir until sugar dissolves. Allow to cool before straining. Store for up to 1 week in a sealed bottle in the fridge.

TOMMY'S MARGARITA

This contemporary classic cocktail was created by Julio Bermejo in the late 80s at his family restaurant, Tommy's, in San Francisco.

50 ML/1⅔ FL OZ. ARETTE REPOSADO TEQUILA

25 ML/¾ FL OZ. FRESH LIME JUICE

15 ML/½ FL OZ. AGAVE NECTAR

LIME WHEELS, TO GARNISH (OPTIONAL)

Add all the drink ingredients to a cocktail shaker with cubed ice and shake vigorously. Double strain into a rocks glass over ice cubes. Garnish with lime wheels.

POMEGRANATE MARGARITA

The pomegranate gives this drink a beautiful pink hue and provides a crisp, dry acidity. Perfect to enjoy poolside or by the beach.

LIME WEDGE AND EQUAL PARTS MIXED WHITE SUGAR AND SEA SALT FLAKES, FOR THE GLASS RIM

50 ML/1⅔ FL OZ. TAPATIO BLANCO TEQUILA

20 ML/⅔ FL OZ. FRESH LIME JUICE

20 ML/⅔ FL OZ. TRIPLE SEC

25 ML/¾ FL OZ. FRESH POMEGRANATE JUICE

FOOD-SAFE ROSE PETALS, TO GARNISH

Rub a lime wedge around the rim of a coupe glass, then dip the outer edge of the rim into the mixed sugar and salt. Shake all the drink ingredients in a cocktail shaker with cubed ice and double strain into the prepared glass. Garnish with a rose petal or two.

ANCHO MARGARITA

A winning combination of tequila, lime, ancho chilli/chile and salt.

LIME WEDGE AND SMOKED SEA SALT FLAKES, FOR THE GLASS RIM

50 ML/1⅔ FL OZ. CABEZA TEQUILA

25 ML/¾ FL OZ. FRESH LIME JUICE

25 ML/¾ FL OZ. ANCHO REYES CHILE LIQUEUR

DEHYDRATED LIME WHEEL, TO GARNISH

Rub the rim of a chilled coupe glass with a lime wedge. Roll the outer edge of the glass rim in the smoked sea salt. Add all the drink ingredients to a cocktail shaker with cubed ice and shake hard. Fine strain into the prepared glass. Garnish with a dehydrated lime wheel.

AL PASTOR MARGARITA

This cocktail was created by Benjamin Padrón Novoa. He was inspired by the traditional spicy *pineapple al pastor* tacos from his native Mexico.

8–10 SMALL CHUNKS OF PINEAPPLE

2–4 FRESH BASIL LEAVES

2–4 FRESH MINT LEAVES

1-CM/½-INCH SLICE OF SERRANO CHILLI/
CHILE (OR ADJUST ACCORDING TO TASTE)

50 ML/1⅔ FL OZ. OCHO BLANCO TEQUILA

25 ML/¾ FL OZ. FRESH LIME JUICE

25 ML/¾ FL OZ. COINTREAU

30 ML/1 FL OZ. PINEAPPLE JUICE

8–10 FRESH CORIANDER/CILANTRO LEAVES

PINEAPPLE LEAVES, TO GARNISH

Muddle the pineapple chunks, fresh herbs and chilli/chile in the base of a cocktail shaker. Add the other drink ingredients and some cubed ice. Shake hard, then double strain into a chilled martini glass. Garnish with three pineapple leaves fanned out.

MEZCARITA

Who doesn't love a blended Margarita? I find this recipe works even better with mezcal than tequila; it adds a pleasant smokiness.

LIME WEDGE AND SMOKED SEA SALT FLAKES,
FOR THE GLASS RIM

50 ML/1⅔ FL OZ. QUIQUIRIQUI MATATLAN
MEZCAL

25 ML/¾ FL OZ. FRESH LIME JUICE

15 ML/½ FL OZ. AGAVE NECTAR

3 DASHES OF PEYCHAUD'S BITTERS

1 LARGE SCOOP OF CUBED ICE

DEHYDRATED BANANA CRISP, TO GARNISH

Prepare a rocks glass by rubbing the rim with a lime wedge, then dip the rim in the smoked sea salt. Blend all the drink ingredients in a blender until they become a consistent 'slushy' texture. Pour the blender contents into the prepared glass. Garnish with a dehydrated banana crisp.

GREENER PASTURES MARGARITA

The avocado gives this blended drink a creamy, smooth texture. Surprisingly easy to drink, it is impossible to have just one of these. Tajin powder is a Mexican seasoning made from a blend of chilli/chili powder, lime and sea salt flakes. If Tajin is unavailable, mix equal parts chilli/chili powder with sea salt flakes.

LIME WEDGE AND TAJÍN POWDER, FOR THE GLASS RIM

50 ML/1⅔ FL OZ. FORTALEZA BLANCO TEQUILA

25 ML/¾ FL OZ. FRESH LIME JUICE

20 ML/⅔ FL OZ. AGAVE NECTAR

HALF A RIPE AVOCADO, PEELED AND PITTED

PINCH OF SEA SALT

3 CORIANDER/CILANTRO SPRIGS

1 LARGE SCOOP OF CUBED ICE

PURPLE EDIBLE FLOWER, TO GARNISH

Rub a lime wedge around the rim of a coupe glass, then dip the outer edge of the rim into the tajin powder. Add all the drink ingredients to a blender and blend until smooth in consistency. Pour the contents of the blender into the prepared glass. Garnish with a purple edible flower.

LONG + REFRESHING

◆

PALOMA

While the Margarita is the most well-known tequila cocktail outside of Mexico, the Paloma is likely the most popular tequila-based mixed drink in Mexico. This drink was popularized by Don Javier Corona Delgado at his bar *La Capilla* in the town of Tequila, who began his bartending career in 1945.

LIME WEDGE AND SEA SALT FLAKES, FOR THE GLASS RIM
50 ML/1⅔ FL OZ. OCHO BLANCO TEQUILA
10 ML/2 TEASPOONS FRESH LIME JUICE
GRAPEFRUIT SODA (SUCH AS SQUIRT, TING OR THREE CENTS), TO TOP UP
FRESH PINK GRAPEFRUIT SLICE, TO GARNISH

Prepare a highball glass by rubbing the rim with a lime wedge, then dip the rim of the glass into the sea salt flakes. Combine all the drink ingredients in the prepared highball glass over cubed ice. Stir to mix and chill the drink. Garnish with a pink grapefruit slice.

HIBISCUS HIGHBALL

Agua de jamaica (hibiscus water) is a popular non-alcoholic drink in Mexico. I've found it makes a beautifully refreshing tequila cocktail.

50 ML/1⅔ FL OZ. CABEZA TEQUILA
25 ML/¾ FL OZ. FRESH LIME JUICE
25 ML/¾ FL OZ. HIBISCUS SYRUP*

SODA WATER, TO TOP UP
EDIBLE FLOWER, TO GARNISH

Add all the drink ingredients to a highball glass over cubed ice. Stir to mix and chill. Garnish the drink with an edible flower.

To make hibiscus syrup: **500 ML/2 CUPS WATER, 500 G/2½ CUPS CASTER/ GRANULATED SUGAR, 75 G/1 CUP DRIED HIBISCUS FLOWERS** Add all the ingredients to a saucepan and bring to a boil. Remove from heat and stir until sugar dissolves. Allow to cool before straining and discarding flowers. Store for up to 1 week in a sealed bottle in the fridge.

MATADOR

I've 'upgraded' this classic cocktail by adding Green Chartreuse. The herbaceous notes complement the vegetal tequila and sweet pineapple.

50 ML/1⅔ FL OZ. OCHO BLANCO TEQUILA
25 ML/¾ FL OZ. FRESH LIME JUICE
30 ML/1 FL OZ. PINEAPPLE JUICE
7.5 ML/1½ TEASPOONS GREEN CHARTREUSE

5 ML/1 TEASPOON AGAVE NECTAR
DEHYDRATED PINEAPPLE SLICE, DEHYDRATED LIME WHEEL AND PINK PEPPERCORNS IN A GRINDER (OPTIONAL), TO GARNISH

Shake the drink ingredients in a cocktail shaker with cubed ice. Strain into a Mexican 'cantarito' or highball glass. Garnish with dehydrated pineapple and lime slices and a grinding of pink peppercorns, if using, to finish.

BATANGA #2

Another of Mexico's most popular drinks, while the original Batanga recipe calls for tequila, lime, salt and Coca-Cola, I prefer this adaptation created by Carl Wrangel at the Barking Dog in Copenhagen. It foregoes Coca-Cola and uses bitter Italian *Amaro* Averna to replicate its flavour.

LIME WEDGE AND SEA SALT FLAKES, FOR THE GLASS RIM

50 ML/1⅔ FL OZ. OCHO BLANCO TEQUILA

25 ML/¾ FL OZ. AVERNA

20 ML/⅔ FL OZ. FRESH LEMON JUICE

25 ML/¾ FL OZ. SIMPLE SUGAR SYRUP

LIME WHEEL, TO GARNISH

Rub the rim of a highball glass with a lime wedge, then dip the rim into the sea salt. Shake all the drink ingredients in a cocktail shaker with cubed ice for 12–15 seconds. Double strain into the prepared glass over cubed ice. Garnish with a lime wheel.

EL DIABLO

This classic tequila cocktail was first featured in *Trader Vic's Book of Food & Drink* under the name 'Mexican El Diablo' (which translates to the 'Mexican Devil'). I have added fresh ginger juice to give it an extra kick.

50 ML/1⅔ FL OZ. OCHO BLANCO TEQUILA

25 ML/¾ FL OZ. FRESH LIME JUICE

10 ML/2 TEASPOONS FRESH GINGER JUICE

20 ML/⅔ FL OZ. SIMPLE SUGAR SYRUP

10 ML/2 TEASPOONS MERLET CRÈME DE CASSIS

FEVER-TREE GINGER ALE, TO TOP UP

LIME WEDGE, TO GARNISH

Add all the drink ingredients, except the ginger ale, to a cocktail shaker with cubed ice, then shake hard. Strain into a highball glass (over ice if preferred) and top up with ginger ale. Garnish with a lime wedge.

LAGERITA

This cocktail combines two of the most refreshing beverages - beer and a Margarita - with fantastic results. Perfect for quenching thirst on a hot summer's day by the beach.

35 ML/1¼ FL OZ. CABEZA TEQUILA
25 ML/¾ FL OZ. FRESH LIME JUICE
20 ML/⅔ FL OZ. AGAVE NECTAR
MEXICAN LAGER, TO TOP UP

Combine all the ingredients in a sling glass over crushed ice. Churn all the ingredients with a bar spoon for around 10-15 seconds, until well mixed.

MEZCAL MULE

A great example of a 'twisted classic' here - the mezcal marries beautifully with the lime and ginger. A cooling drink to enjoy at a midsummer's barbecue.

50 ML/1⅔ FL OZ. DERRUMBES MICHOACÁN MEZCAL
15 ML/½ FL OZ. FRESH LIME JUICE (SAVE A LIME HUSK FOR GARNISH)
PINCH OF SEA SALT
GINGER BEER, TO TOP UP
FRESH MINT SPRIG, TO GARNISH

Add all the drink ingredients to a copper mule mug over cubed ice. Use a bar spoon to churn drink for 10-12 seconds. Garnish with a mint sprig and the used lime husk.

PRIMAVERA PUNCH

This twist on Dick Bradsell's Russian Spring Punch is dangerously drinkable. Raspberries, tequila and Champagne - what's not to love?

50 ML/1⅔ FL OZ. OLMECA ALTOS BLANCO TEQUILA
25 ML/¾ FL OZ. FRESH LIME JUICE
25 ML/¾ FL OZ. RASPBERRY SYRUP*
CHAMPAGNE OR SPARKLING WINE, TO TOP UP
FRESH MINT SPRIG AND FRESH RASPBERRY, TO GARNISH

Combine all ingredients except the Champagne or sparkling wine in a cocktail shaker with cubed ice. Shake and strain into highball glass over cubed ice. Top up with Champagne or sparkling wine. Garnish with a mint sprig and raspberry.

*To make raspberry syrup: 200 G/1½ CUPS FRESH RASPBERRIES, 500 G/2½ CUPS CASTER/GRANULATED SUGAR, 500 ML/2 CUPS BOILING WATER   Muddle the fresh raspberries in the base of a large mixing jug/pitcher. Add the sugar and boiling water and stir until the sugar has dissolved. Allow to cool and then pass the syrup through a fine strainer. Store for up to 1 week in a sealed bottle in the fridge.

ORIGINAL SIN

This cocktail is a testament to just how well tequila and sparkling wine or Champagne can pair. The enticing combination of fresh apple, mint and elderflower liqueur mean that this drink is always a crowd-pleaser.

¼ GRANNY SMITH APPLE, CUBED
6–8 FRESH MINT LEAVES, PLUS MINT SPRIG TO GARNISH
25 ML/¾ FL OZ. CALLE 23 BLANCO TEQUILA
20 ML/⅔ FL OZ. FRESH LIME JUICE

15 ML/½ FL OZ. ST GERMAIN ELDERFLOWER LIQUEUR
10 ML/2 TEASPOONS SIMPLE SUGAR SYRUP
CHAMPAGNE OR SPARKLING WINE, TO TOP UP

Muddle the apple cubes and mint leaves in the base of a cocktail shaker. Add all the other drink ingredients, except the Champagne, to the shaker with cubed ice. Shake and then double strain into a Champagne flute. Top up with Champagne or sparkling wine. Garnish with a mint sprig.

MEXICAN 55

While this drink was originally created by my father, Tomas Estes, in 1988, the specific recipe featured here was adapted by Glenn Morgan at Lab Bar in London.

25 ML/¾ FL OZ. OCHO BLANCO TEQUILA
15 ML/½ FL OZ. FRESH LIME JUICE
5 ML/1 TEASPOON HONEY
10 ML/2 TEASPOONS YELLOW CHARTREUSE

1 DASH OF PIMENTO DRAM
1 DASH OF PEYCHAUD'S BITTERS
CHAMPAGNE, TO TOP UP
PARED LIME ZEST, TO GARNISH

Shake all the drink ingredients, except the Champagne, in a cocktail shaker with cubed ice. Double strain into a chilled champagne flute. Top up with Champagne and garnish with pared lime zest.

BROWN, BITTER + STIRRED

MEZCAL RED HOOK

This spirit-led cocktail packs a serious punch. It is also a great example of how mezcal can replace other spirits in classic cocktails. The original Red Hook is an American whiskey-based cocktail, which itself is a twist on the Sweet Manhattan.

50 ML/1⅔ FL OZ. ILEGAL JOVEN MEZCAL
20 ML/⅔ FL OZ. CARPANO ANTICA FORMULA, OR OTHER SWEET VERMOUTH
10 ML/2 TEASPOONS LUXARDO MARASCHINO LIQUEUR
2 LUXARDO MARASCHINO CHERRIES ON A COCKTAIL STICK, TO GARNISH

Combine all the drink ingredients in a mixing glass with cubed ice. Stir with a bar spoon for 20–30 seconds. Strain into a chilled coupette glass and garnish with the Luxardo maraschino cherries on a cocktail stick.

SMOKING PRESIDENT

The Old Fashioned is enjoying a revival of late, and agave spirits work phenomenally well as the base. Here, the mezcal adds a smoky, oily flavour profile that plays well off of the floral, spicy notes from the bitters and bright citrus flavour of the lemon zest.

60 ML/2 FL OZ. LOS DANZANTES REPOSADO MEZCAL
5 ML/1 TEASPOON AGAVE NECTAR
2 DROPS OF BOB'S LAVENDER BITTERS
2 DROPS OF BOB'S CARDAMOM BITTERS
LEMON ZEST AND FRESH LAVENDER SPRIG, TO GARNISH

Stir all the drink ingredients over cubed ice in a rocks glass for 30-40 seconds, or until the desired level of dilution is reached. Gently squeeze the lemon zest garnish to express the citrus oils into the glass. Garnish the glass with the lemon zest and a lavender sprig.

MESTIZO COCKTAIL

The term *mestizo* is a reference to the Mexican and Latin American population, who have a mixed ethnicity of both indigenous Mesoamerican and European. Here I mix tequila with French and Italian ingredients to create this delicious cocktail.

50 ML/1⅔ FL OZ. OCHO AÑEJO TEQUILA
20 ML/⅔ FL OZ. CARPANO ANTICA FORMULA, OR OTHER SWEET VERMOUTH
5 ML/1 TEASPOON BENEDICTINE
2.5 ML/½ TEASPOON PICON AMER
PARED LEMON ZEST, TO GARNISH

Combine all the drink ingredients in a mixing glass over cubed ice and stir for 20–30 seconds with a bar spoon. Strain into a chilled coupette glass. Gently squeeze the lemon zest garnish to express the citrus oils into the glass before dropping into the drink.

ROSITA

The Rosita is a Negroni with tequila in the place of gin. I find that using Raicilla, another agave spirit from the state of Jalisco, adds creamy, lactic and vegetal notes to this cocktail.

25 ML/¾ FL OZ. LA VENENOSA SUR RAICILLA
25 ML/¾ FL OZ. SWEET VERMOUTH
25 ML/¾ FL OZ. CAMPARI
GRAPEFRUIT SLICES, TO GARNISH

Stir all the drink ingredients over cubed ice in a rocks glass.
Garnish with grapefruit slices.

TEQUILA SAZERAC

Adapted from the classic Sazerac cocktail, in this version the Don Julio 1942's caramel, toffee and chocolate notes play off the aniseed notes of the absinthe to create a moreish sipper.

60 ML/2 FL OZ. DON JULIO 1942 TEQUILA
5 ML/1 TEASPOON AGAVE NECTAR
2 DASHES OF ABSINTHE
3 DASHES OF PEYCHAUD'S BITTERS
LEMON ZEST, TO SERVE

Add all the drink ingredients to a mixing glass with cubed ice and stir for about 30 seconds. Strain into a small chilled rocks glass (no ice). Gently squeeze the lemon zest to express citrus oils over the cocktail and sides of the glass. Discard the zest.

MINISTRY OF LOVE

Created by my cousin and fellow bartender James Estes, this drink is a great example of using both tequila and mezcal as a cocktail base. It is a loose twist on the classic Negroni cocktail, using Italian artichoke-based bitter Cynar (pronounced chee-nar) instead of Campari, and Cocchi Americano instead of sweet vermouth.

15 ML/½ FL OZ. OCHO REPOSADO TEQUILA
15 ML/½ FL OZ. LOS DANZANTES REPOSADO MEZCAL
25 ML/¾ FL OZ. CYNAR
25 ML/¾ FL OZ. COCCHI AMERICANO
5 ML/1 TEASPOON MERLET CRÈME DE CASSIS
5 COFFEE BEANS
PARED LEMON AND ORANGE ZESTS, TO GARNISH

Stir all the drink ingredients in a mixing glass over cubed ice for 20-30 seconds. Single strain into a rocks glass over cubed ice, taking care that the coffee beans do not pass through the strainer. Garnish with lemon and orange zests.

MINT CONDITION

Although this recipe may look unusual on paper, the sum is definitely greater than this cocktail's parts. Tequila's flavour profile lends itself well to mixing with chocolate, which also originated in Mexico (cacao beans are believed to be native to Central America - chocolate can also be found in many traditional Mexican dishes, such as *mole*). I originally created this drink for a food-inspired menu I named 'Food for Thought'; it was designed to taste like a mint chocolate in a glass.

50 ML/1⅔ FL OZ. OCHO REPOSADO TEQUILA

25 ML/¾ FL OZ. CARPANO ANTICA FORMULA, OR OTHER SWEET VERMOUTH

12.5 ML/2½ TEASPOONS MOZART DARK CHOCOLATE LIQUEUR

2.5 ML/½ TEASPOON CRÈME DE MENTHE

2 DASHES OF BITTER TRUTH CHOCOLATE BITTERS

LEMON ZEST, TO SERVE

MINT-FLAVOURED CHOCOLATES (SUCH AS AFTER EIGHTS), TO SERVE

Stir all the drink ingredients in a mixing glass for 25-30 seconds. Strain into a chilled coupette glass. Gently squeeze the lemon zest over the top of the glass to express the citrus oils and discard. Serve with mint-flavoured chocolates (such as After Eights) on the side.

SHORTS, SOURS + SANGRITAS

MEZCAL FIX

Fixes are a forgotten category of drink comprising of a base spirit, citrus juice and pineapple syrup. I have created my own roasted pineapple syrup, added bitter Cynar and a pinch of sea salt. This cocktail contains all five tastes: sweet, sour, bitter, salty and umami (savoury).

40 ML/1⅓ FL OZ. QUIQUIRIQUI MATATLAN MEZCAL
20 ML/⅔ FL OZ. FRESH LIME JUICE
25 ML/¾ FL OZ. ROASTED PINEAPPLE SYRUP*

5 ML/1 TEASPOON CYNAR
PINCH OF SEA SALT
PINEAPPLE LEAF, TO GARNISH (TAKEN FROM PINEAPPLE USED IN SYRUP)

Add all the ingredients to a cocktail shaker with cubed ice and shake hard. Double strain into a pony glass and garnish with a pineapple leaf.

To make pineapple syrup: 1 LARGE PINEAPPLE, 500 ML/2 CUPS WATER, 500 G/2½ CUPS DEMERARA/TURBINADO SUGAR Preheat the oven to 180°C (350°F) Gas 4. Remove pineapple leaves and keep for garnish. Place whole pineapple on a baking tray and roast for 3 hours. Let cool. Cut away skin and core and cut soft flesh into small chunks. Blend to a purée in a blender. Bring the water and sugar to a boil in a saucepan. Remove from heat and stir until sugar dissolves. Bring to a low simmer and add pineapple purée. Stir for 1 minute. Remove from heat and allow to cool before straining. Store for up to 1 week in a sealed bottle in the fridge.

SIESTA

The winning combination of tequila, grapefruit and Campari means that this cocktail is fast becoming a contemporary classic. The Siesta was created by Katie Stipe at Flatiron Lounge in NYC circa 2006.

45 ML/1½ FL OZ. EL TESORO BLANCO TEQUILA
15 ML/½ FL OZ. GRAPEFRUIT JUICE
25 ML/¾ FL OZ. FRESH LIME JUICE

25 ML/¾ FL OZ. SIMPLE SUGAR SYRUP
7.5 ML/1½ TEASPOONS CAMPARI
LIME WHEEL, TO GARNISH

Shake all the drink ingredients in a cocktail shaker with cubed ice. Double strain into a chilled coupe glass. Garnish with a lime wheel.

TINGLET

This award-winning cocktail was created by Megs Miller and has all the makings of a modern classic cocktail; two ingredients, easy to make, and most importantly easy to drink (perhaps a bit too easy).

50 ML/1⅔ FL OZ. OLMECA ALTOS PLATA TEQUILA
30 ML/1 FL OZ. TING CORDIAL*
GRAPEFRUIT ZEST, TO GARNISH

Stir the drink ingredients in a mixing glass for about 30 seconds with cubed ice. Strain into a chilled coupette glass and garnish with grapefruit zest.

To make ting cordial: Add a can of Ting (or other grapefruit soda) to a saucepan over a medium heat. Simmer until volume is halved. Remove cordial from heat and allow to cool. Store for up to 1 week in a sealed bottle in the fridge.

LA ÚLTIMA PALABRA

A twist on the classic gin-based Last Word cocktail… because in my opinion, anything gin can do, mezcal can do better!

25 ML/¾ FL. OZ. SIETE MISTERIOS ESPADÍN MEZCAL

25 ML/¾ FL OZ. FRESH LIME JUICE

25 ML/¾ FL OZ. GREEN CHARTREUSE

25 ML/¾ FL OZ. MARASCHINO LIQUEUR

1 FRESH CORIANDER/CILANTRO SPRIG

DEHYDRATED LIME WHEEL AND FRESH CORIANDER/CILANTRO SPRIG, TO GARNISH

Add all the drink ingredients to a cocktail shaker with cubed ice and shake hard. Double strain into a chilled coupe glass. Float a dehydrated lime wheel on top of the drink and garnish glass with a coriander/cilantro sprig.

RESUCITADOR DE CUERPOS

Another twist on a classic gin cocktail, this time the Corpse Reviver #2. This quaff is remarkably refreshing and dangerously easy to drink.

25 ML/¾ FL OZ. DEL MAGUEY VIDA MEZCAL

25 ML/¾ FL OZ. FRESH LIME JUICE

25 ML/¾ FL OZ. COINTREAU

25 ML/¾ FL OZ. COCCHI AMERICANO (OR LILLET BLANC)

1 DASH OF ABSINTHE

Shake all the drink ingredients in a cocktail shaker with cubed ice. Double strain into a chilled cocktail coupe. No garnish.

PINK CHIHUAHUA

This drink was created by the late, great bartender Dick Bradsell at the eponymous Soho (London) bar. This cocktail is a real crowd-pleaser; even the most tequila-averse won't be able to resist!

50 ML/1⅔ FL OZ. OLMECA ALTOS PLATA TEQUILA
25 ML/¾ FL OZ. FRESH POMEGRANATE JUICE
25 ML/¾ FL OZ. FRESH LIME JUICE

20 ML/⅔ FL OZ. ORGEAT (ALMOND SYRUP)
10 ML/2 TEASPOONS EGG WHITE
LIME WEDGE, TO GARNISH

Add all the drink ingredients to a cocktail shaker and 'dry' shake first without ice. Add cubed ice and shake a second time. Strain into a chilled coupe glass. Garnish with a lime wedge on the rim of the glass.

NAKED & FAMOUS

This drink was created by Joaquín Simó in late 2010 at Death & Company in NYC. In his own words, 'This Oaxacan riff on a Last Word tempers mezcal's funky smokiness with a honeyed alpine herbal liqueur, citrusy amaro and fresh lime juice.'

25 ML/¾ FL OZ. DEL MAGUEY CHICHICAPA MEZCAL
25 ML/¾ FL OZ. FRESH LIME JUICE
25 ML/¾ FL OZ. YELLOW CHARTREUSE
25 ML/¾ FL OZ. APEROL

Combine all the drink ingredients in a cocktail shaker with cubed ice and shake hard. Double strain into a chilled coupe glass. No garnish.

CLASSIC SANGRITA

In Mexico, neat tequila is traditionally served alongside Sangrita, which translates to 'little blood.' Over time, recipes have evolved to include tomato juice, though original recipes likely did not. Think of it as a small portion of a Virgin Mary. This recipe makes about fifteen small servings.

200 ML/6¾ FL OZ. TOMATO OR CLAMATO JUICE

200 ML/6¾ FL OZ. FRESH ORANGE JUICE

200 ML/6¾ FL OZ. FRESH POMEGRANATE JUICE

100 ML/3½ FL OZ. FRESH LIME JUICE

2 TEASPOONS MALDON SEA SALT

1 TEASPOON CRACKED BLACK PEPPER

50 ML/1⅔ FL OZ. CHOLULA HOT SAUCE (OR ADJUST TO TASTE)

Add all the drink ingredients to a jug/pitcher and stir until evenly combined. Store in a sealed bottle in the fridge for up to 5 days.

VERDITA

This fresh, bright twist on a Sangrita was likely introduced to the UK by Dré Masso and Henry Besant at their tequila bar, Green & Red, in London. This recipe makes about ten small servings.

1 HANDFUL OF CORIANDER/CILANTRO LEAVES

½ HANDFUL OF FRESH MINT LEAVES

3 GREEN JALAPEÑOS (OR SCALE BACK IF YOU WANT LESS SPICE)

500 ML/2 CUPS PINEAPPLE JUICE

LARGE PINCH OF SEA SALT FLAKES

Put all the drink ingredients in a blender and process until well blended. Fine strain before storing in a sealed bottle in the fridge for up to 5 days.

FOR THE ADVENTUROUS

◆

UNDER THE VOLCANO

Named after the eponymous novel by Malcolm Lowry, in which the 'Consul' famously drinks himself to death in Mexico, this cocktail is smooth and refreshing but packs a deceptively strong punch!

50 ML/1⅔ FL OZ. MARCA NEGRA ESPADÍN MEZCAL

25 ML/¾ FL OZ. FRESH LEMON JUICE

25 ML/¾ FL OZ. GREEN TEA SYRUP*

3 DASHES OF ABSINTHE

20 ML/⅔ FL OZ. EGG WHITE

SODA WATER, TO TOP UP

STAR ANISE, ABSINTHE AND LIME ZEST, TO GARNISH

Add all the drink ingredients, except the soda water, to a cocktail shaker. Shake vigorously for 15–20 seconds, then single strain into a highball glass over cubed ice. Top up with soda water. For the garnish, soak a star anise in absinthe, carefully light on fire in a teaspoon and place over the top of strips of lime zest in the glass.

To make green tea syrup: 2 TABLESPOONS LOOSE-LEAF GREEN TEA (OR 2 TEA BAGS), 200 G/1 CUP CASTER/GRANULATED SUGAR, 230 ML/1 CUP WATER

Combine the tea, sugar and water in a saucepan. Bring to a boil, stirring frequently. Simmer for about 2 minutes. Remove from heat, cover and stand for 2 minutes. Let cool before straining. Store for up to 1 week in a sealed bottle in the fridge.

TEQUILA COLADA

Jake Burger has managed to improve on the tried-and-true classic Piña Colada - replacing rum with tequila, which he serves at his London tequila bar Cielo Blanco. This is perfect for sipping at the beach... and if you're not by the beach - well, this cocktail is the next best thing.

35 ML/1¼ FL OZ. OCHO BLANCO TEQUILA

25 ML/¾ FL OZ. EL YUCATECO HORCHATA CONCENTRATE

25 ML/¾ FL OZ. COCO LOPEZ

15 ML/½ FL OZ. MANZANILLA SHERRY

8 CUBES OF FRESH PINEAPPLE

A SCOOP OF THE 'MEAT' FROM A FRESH YOUNG COCONUT

1 LARGE SCOOP OF CUBED ICE

PINCH OF SEA SALT

PINEAPPLE LEAF, TO GARNISH

Blend all the drink ingredients until smooth. Pour out the contents of the blender into an empty coconut or a mason jar. Garnish with a pineapple leaf.

NO MANCHES!

Created by Alain Branco at Pistola y Corazón tequila bar in Lisbon, this rich combination of ingredients is ideal as a postprandial sipper.

50 ML/1⅔ FL OZ. SAN COSME MEZCAL

60 ML/2 FL OZ. FRESH POMEGRANATE JUICE

35 ML/1¼ FL OZ. FRESH LEMON JUICE

35 ML/1¼ FL OZ. EGG WHITE

25 ML/¾ FL OZ. VANILLA GOMME SYRUP

PINCH OF SEA SALT

4 DASHES OF CHOLULA OR VALENTINA HOT SAUCE

1 CHILE DE ÁRBOL, TO GARNISH

Add all the drink ingredients to a cocktail shaker. 'Dry' shake without ice first to emulsify egg white. Add ice and shake a second time. Double strain into a chilled coupe glass. Garnish with a chile de árbol.

RAGS TO RICHES

This twist on the Old Fashioned plays on the sweet, nutty
and creamy notes found in Herradura Reposado tequila.
It is a moreish tipple to sip over dessert.

60 ML/2 FL OZ. HERRADURA REPOSADO TEQUILA, FAT-WASHED WITH HAZELNUT
BROWN BUTTER*
6 ML/GENEROUS 1 TEASPOON SIMPLE SUGAR SYRUP
3 DASHES OF ANGOSTURA BITTERS
LEMON AND ORANGE ZESTS, TO GARNISH

Stir all the drink ingredients over cubed ice in a rocks glass for about 30 seconds.
Garnish with lemon and orange zests.

To make fat-washed tequila: 100 G/1 STICK UNSALTED BUTTER,
1 HANDFUL OF CRUSHED HAZELNUTS, 700 ML/3 CUPS HERRADURA REPOSADO TEQUILA
Heat the butter in a small saucepan over a medium heat until it starts to bubble
and 'brown'. Add the crushed hazelnuts, remove the pan from the heat and stir
continuously for 1 minute. Add the butter and hazelnut mixture to a jug/pitcher
containing the Herradura Reposado tequila and stir. Let cool for an hour before
placing in the freezer overnight. Strain out the solids the next day and store the
tequila in a sealed bottle at room temperature for 2 weeks.

BLUE DAISY

The deep turquoise colour provides a pleasant backdrop while sipping on this cocktail… one could even imagine they are gazing out across the ocean in the Mayan Riviera.

45 ML/1½ FL OZ. CURADO TEQUILA
15 ML/½ FL OZ. FRESH LIME JUICE
25 ML/¾ FL OZ. PINEAPPLE JUICE

15 ML/½ FL OZ. BLUE CURAÇAO
10 ML/2 TEASPOONS LUXARDO MARASCHINO LIQUEUR
FRESH ROSEMARY SPRIG, TO GARNISH

Shake all the drink ingredients very hard with cubed ice in a cocktail shaker, then double strain into a chilled coupe glass. Use a match to slightly burn the end of the rosemary sprig to release the aromas, before garnishing the top of the cocktail.

DEATH FLIP

Created by Chris Hysted-Adams in 2010 at the world-famous Black Pearl bar in Melbourne, the drink originally bore the following menu description: 'You don't wanna meet this cocktail in a dark alley. Ingredients unnamed.' While it may initially sound like a strange mix of ingredients, trust me: try this drink!

30 ML/1 FL OZ. OCHO BLANCO TEQUILA
15 ML/½ FL OZ. YELLOW CHARTREUSE
15 ML/½ FL OZ. JÄGERMEISTER

5 ML/1 TEASPOON VANILLA GOMME SYRUP
1 WHOLE EGG
FRESHLY GRATED NUTMEG, TO GARNISH

Add all the drink ingredients to a cocktail shaker with cubed ice. Shake long and hard to emulsify the egg. Fine strain into a chilled coupette glass. Garnish with freshly grated nutmeg over half of the cocktail.

HORCHATA BORRACHA

Horchata is a traditional *agua fresca* in Mexico and is normally served without alcohol. However, the cinnamon, cream and vanilla notes play off of the Reposado tequila beautifully.

ORANGE WEDGE AND GROUND CINNAMON, FOR THE GLASS RIM
50 ML/1⅔ FL OZ. DON FULANO REPOSADO TEQUILA
120 ML/4 FL OZ. HORCHATA*
PURPLE EDIBLE FLOWER, TO GARNISH

Rub the rim of a highball glass with an orange wedge, then dip the rim in ground cinnamon. Add all the drink ingredients to the prepared glass over cubed ice. Stir the drink for 10–15 seconds. Garnish with a purple edible flower.

* *To make horchata:* 500 G/2½ CUPS LONG-GRAIN WHITE RICE, 1 LITRE/ 4 CUPS WATER, 2 CINNAMON STICKS, SEEDS FROM 1 VANILLA POD/BEAN, 400-G/14-OZ. CAN OF CONDENSED MILK, 400-G/14-OZ. CAN OF EVAPORATED MILK Soak the rice in the water for 3–4 hours. Place the soaked rice and water in a blender with the cinnamon sticks, vanilla seeds, condensed milk and evaporated milk. Blend all ingredients on high until smooth. Pour the liquid slowly through muslin/cheesecloth or a fine-mesh strainer to strain out all the solids. Store in a sealed bottle in the fridge for up to 1 week.

TEQUILA BEYOND SUNRISE

The cocktail that this book is named after, the Tequila Sunrise, while widely recognized, I feel is somewhat outdated and is not the most balanced cocktail. As such I have updated the recipe to something I feel is more in line with modern palates and contemporary drinking.

45 ML/1½ FL OZ. OCHO REPOSADO TEQUILA

60 ML/2 FL OZ. FRESH ORANGE JUICE

15 ML/½ FL OZ. FRESH LIME JUICE

10 ML/2 TEASPOONS SIMPLE SUGAR SYRUP

10 ML/2 TEASPOONS EGG WHITE

5 ML/1 TEASPOON YUZU JUICE

PINCH OF SEA SALT

15 ML/½ FL OZ. POMEGRANATE, PORT AND CHIPOTLE REDUCTION*

ORANGE ZEST, LUXARDO MARASCHINO CHERRY AND COCKTAIL STICK, TO GARNISH

Add all the drink ingredients, except the pomegranate reduction, to a cocktail shaker with cubed ice. Shake very hard and strain into a highball glass over cubed ice. Add the pomegranate, port and chipotle reduction - it will gently sink to the bottom to give the 'sunrise' look. Garnish with an orange zest and cherry 'flag'.

*To make pomegranate reduction: 500 ML/2 CUPS FRESHLY SQUEEZED POMEGRANATE JUICE, 500 ML/2 CUPS RUBY PORT, 500 G/2½ CUPS LIGHT BROWN MUSCOVADO SUGAR, 2 TEASPOONS CHIPOTLE CHILLI/CHILI POWDER Add the pomegranate juice and port to a saucepan and simmer for about 45 minutes until reduced by half. Add the sugar and chilli/chili powder and stir until dissolved. Remove from the heat and allow to cool. Store in a sealed bottle in the fridge for up to 2 weeks.

CREDITS

The author and the publishers would like to thank all the suppliers who so generously supplied their wonderful tequilas used in the drinks and photography for this book.

Cask Liquid Marketing
www.caskliquidmarketing.com
Ocho Blanco, Ocho Reposado, Ocho Añejo, QuiQuiRiQui Matatlan, Tequila Cabeza, Tequila Curado

Indie Brands
www.indiebrands.co.uk
Arette Reposado, Fortaleza Blanco

Speciality Spirits
www.specialityspirits.co.uk
Ilegal Joven, Tapatio Blanco, Mezcal Derrumbes Michoacan, Don Fulano Reposado, La Venenosa Sur Raicilla

Amathus Drinks
www.amathusdrinks.com
Calle 23 Banco, Los Danzantes Reposado, Siete Misterios Espadin, Del Maguey Vida, Del Maguey Chichicapa

Diageo
www.diageo.com
Don Julio 1942

Spirit Cartel
www.spiritcartel.com
Mezcal San Cosme

Mangrove
www.mangroveuk.com
Herradura Reposado

10 Degrees
www.10degreesc.com
Marca Negra Espadin

Pernod Ricard
www.pernod-ricard.com
Altos Blanco

ACKNOWLEDGMENTS

Thanks to all the bartenders who gave me permission to use their cocktail recipes in the book: Alain Branco, Anton Regnéll, Bea and Dick Bradsell, Benjamin Padrón Novoa, Carl 'Blondie' Wrangel, Chris Hysted-Adams, Dré Masso, Jake Burger, James Estes, Joaquin Simó, Julio Bermejo, Katie Stipe, Megs Miller and Tomas Estes. Special thanks to Tristan Stephenson for putting me in touch with his publishers, Ryland Peters & Small. Last but not least, I owe a debt of gratitude to Charmaine Ann Thio for coming up with the perfect name for the book, *Tequila Beyond Sunrise*!

INDEX